T0197528

Emily Walks the Sheep Trail

Cindy Shanks

© 2010 Cindy Shanks. All rights reserved.

No part of this book may be reproduced, stored in a retrieval system, or transmitted by any means without the written permission of the author.

AuthorHouse™
1663 Liberty Drive
Bloomington, IN 47403
www.authorhouse.com
Phone: 833-262-8899

Because of the dynamic nature of the Internet, any web addresses or links contained in this book may have changed since publication and may no longer be valid. The views expressed in this work are solely those of the author and do not necessarily reflect the views of the publisher, and the publisher hereby disclaims any responsibility for them.

Any people depicted in stock imagery provided by Getty Images are models, and such images are being used for illustrative purposes only. Certain stock imagery © Getty Images.

This book is printed on acid-free paper.

ISBN: 978-1-4490-2208-2 (sc)

Library of Congress Control Number: 2009909338

Print information available on the last page.

Published by AuthorHouse 05/27/2021

authorHOUSE®

My name is Emily and I was born in an alfalfa field, on a farm near Florence, Arizona. My mom had been grazing in the mountains of Northern Arizona all summer. She walked 45 days on the Heber-Reno Sheep Trail to graze in the warm desert during the winter. I was born in October, when mom reached the farm. And that is where my story starts.

I belong to the Sheep Springs Sheep Co. which is owned by the Dobson family. I was born with a twin brother. The herders who took care of us hobbled us together as soon as we were born to make sure that our mom fed both of us. We learned to eat, sleep, walk and run together. It was fun to always have my brother close by.

When we were one week old, Hugo came into the field with his shepherd's staff. He used his hook to catch us and then took off our leather hobbles. He wrote numbers on our backs with a big black marker. Then he clipped two little notches in both of my ears. It was like getting my ears pierced. The notches remind the herders that I am a girl twin and will be a mom someday.

Every day I played with my friends, racing and jumping in the field. Mom was always close by, eating or resting with other ewes (moms). I started to eat alfalfa soon after I was born. Mom showed me how to drink water from the big tanks in the field when I was tall enough. I still drank my mom's milk until I was almost four months old.

Our herders worked hard every day to keep us healthy and safe. When we moved to a fresh field of alfalfa, the herders built new electric fences to protect us from the coyotes. They also made sure our water tanks were filled.

If we were sick, the herders took us to the corrals where Solomon took care of us. Sometimes new lambs needed special care, so they stayed in the corrals until they could eat alfalfa in the fields. Solomon also took care of the mother ewes when they were sick.

When we were born, our tails were very long. They had to be docked, or shortened, to keep us clean and healthy. The day the herders rounded us up to dock our tails was a very busy day. Demetrio or Diercio carried us to Felipe who gave us a tetanus shot in our shoulder.

Froylan checked our eyes to see if we had pink eye. He sprayed medicine in our eyes if it was needed. Then he docked our tails. It didn't hurt very much. Abel sprayed our new short tails with medicine so we wouldn't get infected.

Hugo branded us with paint. All of the ewes were branded with an H or a D. These brands belong to Sheep Springs Sheep Co. A number brand on the lambs told the herders which flock we belonged to. The first lambs born at the farm were branded H 1, so they were the oldest. My letter was H and my number was 7.

Winter was a busy time at the farm. There were days when as many as 100 lambs were born. When the lambs were about five months old, most of them were loaded into big trucks and taken to market. A white ewe lamb born as a twin stayed with their mom to walk the trail. They would be the new mothers next winter.

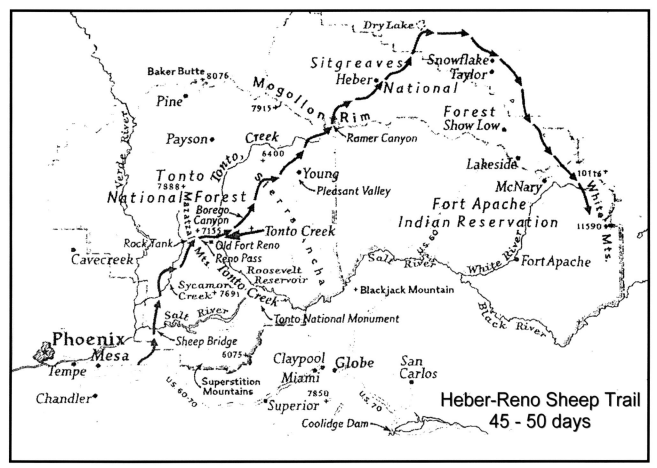

When the weather started getting warmer in the desert, it was time to move north to cooler grazing lands. Bands of 2000 sheep have walked the Heber-Reno Sheep Trail (or driveway) for over 100 years. The Dobson sheep are the last two bands still walking the 220 miles to the mountains near Greer, Arizona. The desert is too hot for woolly ewes in the summer, so they leave the valley in April. The mountains are too cold in the winter for the lambs to be born, so the ewes return to the desert in October. The trail takes 45-50 days each way, and is not easy for the sheep or the herders.

One morning Mark, the manager of the Dobson sheep, brought three big white trucks to the farm. We were loaded into the trucks for the short ride to a grazing field near Signal Butte Road. We spent the night there while the herders got ready to begin the long trail.

At sunrise on Saturday morning, we left the field and crossed under Highway 60. We walked slowly up the middle of Signal Butte Road. First in line was a police car with bright, flashing lights. Then Dwayne Dobson followed in his big, white truck. Felipe, the foreman, walked next leading the band of 2000 sheep. The herders and their dogs walked on both sides of the road to make sure that we stayed together and kept moving. Mark drove his truck behind the sheep and picked up any ewes that were having trouble walking. Last in the long line was another police car with its bright lights flashing too. We walked four miles to a desert field near Brown Road and stopped to rest for the night.

Day two of the trail was our first day of walking in fields of cactus. The trail led us into Usery Mountain Park. We filled the main road as we walked through the park. All the people along the road smiled and waited patiently for us to pass. We went out the main gate and into the desert to spend the night in Bulldog Canyon. Another band of 2000 ewes followed one day behind us all along the trail.

The morning of day three, we walked through Bulldog Canyon to the Lower Salt River. The supplies for the herders were brought to camp in wooden boxes, and small barrels carried their water. A horse and seven burros also arrived. The burros would carry all the food, water and supplies for the herder and the campero. Chagua was our campero. He rode his horse on the trail ahead of the sheep. He set up camp twice a day, packed and unpacked the burros and prepared the meals. Our herder Demetrio and his dog Tigre walked the trail behind us, usually in a thick cloud of dust. He kept us moving and made sure we were safe and healthy.

Day four was a busy day. Chagua saddled his horse and the burros were packed with the supplies. We crossed the Blue Point Bridge just after sunrise. The burros walked in front with Chagua's dog, Duke. Chagua followed on his horse.

We all followed Chagua, 2000 baaing sheep. The bridge was filled with white, woolly faces and the sounds of 8000 small hooves tapping on the concrete. There were lots of friendly people who waved and took pictures. Demetrio and Tigre walked behind us as we crossed the bridge.

When we reached the end of the bridge, we ran onto the sandy beach, raising a thick cloud of dust. We stopped at the base of the mountain and waited patiently for Chagua, Duke, the horse and the burros to lead us down the path. We followed them onto the narrow ledge that hugged the mountain.

We walked in single file onto the narrow trail. Felipe sat high on a rock to count each of us as we passed. His count was called a census and was very important because Sheep Springs Sheep Co. paid a grazing fee for every sheep that walked through forest service land.

As we walked along the path next to the river, I could hear bells ringing. Some of the older ewes wore the bells to help us find our way. Since this was my first time on the trail, I was glad to hear the bells. I knew that I would not get lost if I followed their sound. I stayed very close to mom because she had been on this trail before, and I knew she would teach me what to do. Maybe next year I would be chosen to wear a bell, too.

We walked up through a narrow canyon and over small hills to our resting place. When we got there, I was glad to find a little shade and some grass to eat. Our herders hobbled the burros and tied the horse to a tree. They built a fire and cooked their lunch.

After lunch and clean-up was siesta time. We all rested until the air was cooler. Siesta time was my favorite part of the trail. Then the burros were repacked, the horse was saddled and we started our afternoon walk. We crossed under the Beeline Highway and walked towards Sugarloaf Mountain.

The desert was a hard place to walk. The cactus poked us with prickly spines and the jagged rocks hurt our hooves. Each day we walked three miles in the morning and then took our siesta. We walked another three miles in the afternoon and then stopped for the night. Sometimes we had to walk for two or three days before we found water. But, my mom told me that each day we moved closer to cooler weather and meadows of green grass.

After walking through the desert for nine days, we arrived at Bushnell Tanks. We enjoyed cool spring water from the large tanks. From there we had three hard, rocky days of walking over Reno Pass to reach the waters of Tonto Creek. We walked down from the mountain pass through a wide, green valley. We could see the highway ahead.

We followed the horse and burros into a dark tunnel that went under Highway 188 near Punkin Center. Felipe was waiting at the end of the tunnel to count us again. As we came out of the tunnel into the bright sunlight, we jumped with excitement because we could smell the water. We ran through the dusty sand to Tonto Creek. We needed a long, cool drink of water.

My mom said that some years the creek was deep and she had to swim across. But this year it was an easy walk through shallow water. We enjoyed the green grass along the bank and the fresh, running water. Mom said there were many more days of desert ahead.

After crossing Tonto Creek, we began to move towards the Sierra Anchas Mountains. We were still walking in desert heat as well as facing dangerous desert animals. We saw scorpions, tarantulas, Gila monsters and rattlesnakes. At night we were in danger from coyotes and mountain lions. We walked for nine days through the desert, across mesas, and finally into the cool pine trees at the top of the mountains. We found water in canyons and streams along the trail.

When we reached Walnut Creek, Felipe and Froylan were waiting with salt for us, and fresh supplies and water for the herders. We drank cool water from the creek and enjoyed the grass that had replaced the dry desert grazing. A few miles walk led us to Pleasant Valley mesas where we stopped for a few days. We needed time to rest our hooves and bodies, and feed on the spring grass.

We grazed near the town of Young in Pleasant Valley. This was where the cattlemen and sheep men had one of the deadliest range wars ever fought in the west. Two families started the fight over grasslands and water rights. The shooting between the Graham and the Tewksbury families began in the 1880s. They fought for almost ten years until there were no men in the families left to fight. More than 20 men were killed before the war finally stopped. Today, Young is a very quiet, peaceful place in a beautiful valley.

After resting a few days, we climbed up through a wide, steep canyon to the top of the Mogollon Rim near Forest Lakes. Felipe, Abel and Froylan stopped the cars and trucks on Highway 260 so we could follow Chagua, his horse and the burros across the highway and into the tall trees.

Demetrio and Tigre led us through forests that smelled of pine trees, and meadows of tall, green grass. We were glad to be in cooler weather. We walked for days through the forest with lots of grass to eat and water for drinking.

It began to rain almost every day and we were soon covered in mud. Our brands began to wash from our fleece. All of the animals that walked with us hated the rain. Our herders wore yellow slickers (raincoats) to protect them from the water.

After crossing the road near Dry Lake, we left the trees and walked through high desert woodlands for a week. It was warm during the day and cool at night. Sometimes it rained in the afternoon. We walked on private land around Snowflake and Taylor before we reached the Apache-Sitgreaves National Forest.

Rams (dads) were added to our band of sheep the last few days of the trail. Some of the rams had black faces, but my dad was all white with very long, curly horns. I thought he was very handsome. Mark trucked the rams to the mountains to breed with the ewes during the summer. They walked the last few miles with us. When we saw the aspens and pine trees, mom told me we were close to the grasslands that would be our summer home.

We were near the end of the long trail. The older ewes smelled salt that had been poured onto the ground for us. They began making loud baaing noises that echoed in the tall trees. We all began to make noises of excitement. It sounded like a very large hive of bees. The sheep in the front began running and we all followed. As we rounded the corner of trees, we saw the herders blocking the opening in the fence. Felipe needed to count us again. We waited as patiently as we could for our turn, and then we ran to the field to eat the salt.

A short walk through the trees led us to the old herder's cabins. The supply boxes and water barrels had been unloaded, the burros were hobbled and the horse tied to a tree. We were taken to graze in the tall aspen trees nearby. Our long trail had ended and our cool summer in the mountains had begun.

The next day we woke up to noisy activity in the corrals across the road. We saw men setting up machines in a big tent. It was time for shearing. My mom was glad that she was going to have her heavy wool cut off for summer. After crossing the highway, some of us were led into the corrals. The rest of the herd went to graze. As we moved towards the tent, Felipe opened the gate for me to go into the open field. I didn't have enough wool to be sheared yet. I tried not to be too disappointed.

My mom was led to a shearer who laid her down on the ground and sheared off all of her wool very quickly. (She looked really skinny and I laughed). She was moved out into a corral where Froylan branded her, Abel gave her a shot and Chagua checked her for ticks and worms. Then she was sent to the field to graze.

We spent our summer days eating tall, green grass and resting. At night we were herded into a corral with an electric fence. This protected us from the wolves and coyotes. We walked to new grass every three or four days. Felipe moved the herder's trailer and built fences near our new grazing land.

Sometimes Felipe, Abel and Froylan brought us corn to make us stronger. That was a special treat that we all really liked. They also brought salt. Felipe brought food and water for the herders and the dogs. He made sure we were all taken care of and stayed healthy and safe.

The dogs were very important to the herders. When the herder would whistle or point, the dogs would round us up and move us. They worked very hard on the trail to make sure we all stayed together and were safe. They kept us walking when we moved to a new field, and they moved us into our corral at night. We had a big white dog that stayed with us all of the time. He was named Blue because he wore a blue collar. He watched for danger and was our guardian dog. The herding dogs, named Duke and Tigre, slept near the herders.

After ten weeks in the mountains, it was time to start the trail back to the valley.   It was starting to get cooler and soon the snow would arrive. We needed to go back to the valley to have our new lambs and graze the alfalfa fields during the warm winter months. In the middle of August, the herders began packing. The burros and horses were brought back to the old herder's cabins. We were ready to start the trail back to the farm.

We followed the Heber-Reno Sheep Trail south. We walked for 45 days until we reached the Salt River. The water was very shallow so we walked through the water instead of going across the bridge. We walked three more days through Bulldog Canyon, Usery Mountain Park and down Signal Butte Road. We were trucked the last few miles back to the farm.

I am very excited to be back at the farm. The alfalfa tastes rich and good. I am going to have my first lamb in a few weeks. I want to have twins just like my mom. Maybe next year I will be the mom walking with her lamb ewe. I hope I get to wear a bell.

Acknowledgements

I sincerely want to thank Dwayne Dobson for his enthusiasm in my endeavor to tell the story of the Heber-Reno Sheep Trail. I greatly appreciate his support in allowing me free access to the farm and the ranch of Sheep Springs Sheep Co. Special thanks to Mark (manager) and Felipe (foreman) for including me in the day to day operations of sheep ranching, and allowing me to follow them around with my camera.   Muchas gracias to the herders who have allowed me to document their lives for a year.

The Heber-Reno Sheep Trail is a designated sheep driveway that has been in existence since the 1880s. Most of the trail passes through National Forest Land which belongs to the American people. This is our heritage. The government felt that it was important to protect this corridor of safe land for seasonal sheep migration. President Woodrow Wilson signed an executive order in 1916 making the Arizona driveways the only legalized stock driveways in America. History continues to walk through Arizona with each band of 2000 sheep who travel the trail.

Dwayne Dobson

Mark Pedersen

Printed in the United States
by Baker & Taylor Publisher Services